# The Pest
# with a Vest

**Anders Hanson**

Consulting Editor, Diane Craig, M.A./Reading Specialist

ABDO
Publishing Company

Published by ABDO Publishing Company, 4940 Viking Drive, Edina, Minnesota 55435.

Printed in the United States.

Credits
Edited by: Pam Price
Curriculum Coordinator: Nancy Tuminelly
Cover and Interior Design and Production: Mighty Media
Photo Credits: AbleStock, Comstock, Photodisc

Library of Congress Cataloging-in-Publication Data

Hanson, Anders, 1980-
     The pest with a vest / Anders Hanson.
          p. cm. -- (First rhymes)
     Includes index.
     ISBN 1-59679-503-4 (hardcover)
     ISBN 1-59679-504-2 (paperback)
          1. English language--Rhyme--Juvenile literature. I. Title. II. Series.
     PE1517H37837 2005
     808.1--dc22

                                                                    2005048554

SandCastle™ books are created by a professional team of educators, reading specialists, and content developers around five essential components that include phonemic awareness, phonics, vocabulary, text comprehension, and fluency. All books are written, reviewed, and leveled for guided reading and early intervention reading, and designed for use in shared, guided, and independent reading and writing activities to support a balanced approach to literacy instruction.

# Let Us Know

After reading the book, SandCastle would like you to tell us your stories about reading. What is your favorite page? Was there something hard that you needed help with? Share the ups and downs of learning to read. We want to hear from you! To get posted on the ABDO Publishing Company Web site, send us e-mail at:

**sandcastle@abdopub.com**

**SandCastle Level: Beginning**

# -est

chest

nest

pest

test

vest

3

I look at the .

See the .

This is a  .

I look at the .

We look at a .

The chest is old.

The nest is round.

The bug is a pest.

# The test was hard.

# The vest is tan.

# The Pest
# with a Vest

Pete is a pest.

Pete the pest
lives in a nest.

Pete the pest
has a chest
in his nest.

The chest in the nest
is where Pete the pest
keeps his best vest.

When Pete the pest
leaves his nest
to take a big test,
he gets his best vest
out of the chest.

# About SandCastle™

A professional team of educators, reading specialists, and content developers created the SandCastle™ series to support young readers as they develop reading skills and strategies and increase their general knowledge. The SandCastle™ series has four levels that correspond to early literacy development in young children. The levels are provided to help teachers and parents select the appropriate books for young readers.

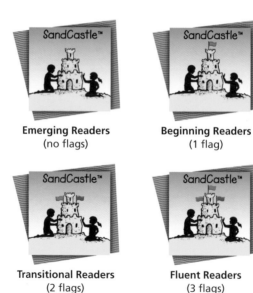

**Emerging Readers**
(no flags)

**Beginning Readers**
(1 flag)

**Transitional Readers**
(2 flags)

**Fluent Readers**
(3 flags)

These levels are meant only as a guide. All levels are subject to change.

**ABDO**
**Publishing Company**

To see a complete list of SandCastle™ books and other nonfiction titles from ABDO Publishing Company, visit www.abdopub.com or contact us at:
4940 Viking Drive, Edina, Minnesota 55435 • 1-800-800-1312 • fax: 1-952-831-1632